J796.42 MAC
Macht, Norman L.
The composite guide to
 track & field /
Colleyville PL

WITHDRAWN

D1090454

THE COMPOSITE GUIDE

IN THIS SERIES

THE COMPOSITE GUIDE

to **TRACK & FIELD**

NORMAN L. MACHT

CHELSEA HOUSE PUBLISHERS

Philadelphia

WITHDRAWN

Colleyville Public Library
110 Main Street
Colleyville, TX 76034

Produced by Choptank Syndicate, Inc.

Editor and Picture Researcher: Norman L. Macht
Production Coordinator and Editorial Assistant: Mary E. Hull
Design and Production: Lisa Hochstein
Cover Illustrator: Cliff Spohn
Cover Design: Keith Trego
Art Direction: Sara Davis

© 1999 by Chelsea House Publishers,
a subsidiary of Haights Cross Communications.
Printed and bound in the United States of America.

3 5 7 9 8 6 4

Library of Congress Cataloging-in-Publication Data

Macht, Norman L. (Norman Lee), 1929-
        The composite guide to track & field / Norman L. Macht.
            p.   cm.— (The composite guide)
        Includes bibliographical references (p.) and index.
        Summary: Surveys the history of track and field competitions from their origins
    in ancient Greece to the accomplishments of top athletes in the twentieth century.
        ISBN 0-7910-4720-2
        1. Track athletics—History—Juvenile literature.
        2. Track and field athletes—Biography—Juvenile literature.
        [1. Track and field—History.] I. Title. II. Series.
    GV1060.5.M25 1998
    796.42—dc21   97-47684
                                                              CIP
                                                              AC

CONTENTS

THE WORLD'S GREATEST ATHLETE

The drums of war in Europe were beginning to drown out the Olympics' message of peaceful competition as the athletes assembled in Berlin, Germany in April 1936. The German dictator, Adolf Hitler, had begun to threaten neighboring nations and had launched his campaign against German Jews, which would force them out of their homes and businesses and lead to the Holocaust.

Loudly trumpeting the superiority of the Aryan, a term he applied to blond-haired northern Europeans, Hitler considered blacks inferior and ridiculed the American team for relying on black athletes to win medals for the United States.

Many Americans opposed sending a team to Berlin. They preferred to boycott the Games as a protest against Hitler's persecution of German citizens and his threats to other European nations. Black newspapers had another reason for urging black athletes to stay home. They did not want to see them representing a country where major league baseball and professional football would not let them play.

In this atmosphere, 12 black track and field teammates set sail for Germany with the rest of the U.S. Olympic team on April 15, 1936. One of them was Jesse Owens, called by a black newspaper "without a doubt the greatest individual performer the world has ever seen."

Owens was no stranger to racial hostility from whites or criticism from blacks. He was

After winning four gold medals at the 1936 Olympics in Germany, Jesse Owens described the secret of his speed: "I let my feet spend as little time on the ground as possible. From the air, fast down, and from the ground, fast up. My foot is only a fraction of the time on the track."

born James Cleveland Owens on September 12, 1913, in Danville, Alabama. His parents were sharecroppers; his grandparents had been slaves. Sharecroppers raised what they could on stingy land they did not own, paying a share of the crop as rent. One of nine children who survived, J. C., as he was called by his family, started working in the fields as soon as he could walk. By the age of seven, he was picking 100 pounds of cotton a day.

Young J. C. was sickly. The winter winds blew through the cracks in his family's cabin and gave him chronic bronchitis. Mysterious growths appeared on his chest and legs.

Poor blacks in the south lived in a world of discrimination and segregation. But J. C.'s parents did not cultivate bitterness or hatred in their children. They were powerless to change the way things were, but they did not have to stay. In 1922 the family moved to Cleveland, Ohio.

When nine-year-old James went to his new elementary school, the teacher asked him his name. "J. C.," he mumbled shyly. The teacher thought he said, "Jesse," so Owens went on the school roll and eventually into the history books as Jesse Owens.

Jesse quickly discovered that he could run faster and jump farther than the other kids. He impressed the physical education teacher, Charles Riley, who began to work with him in developing his athletic skills. By the time Jesse was 15, he had set world records for his age by clearing six feet in the high jump and almost 23 feet in the long jump. He also played on the school basketball team.

In high school Jesse tied or broke world records in the 100- and 220-yard dashes. When he graduated and enrolled at Ohio State University in nearby Columbus, Jesse drew harsh criticism from Cleveland's black press. He knew the university was segregated; he and the few other black students could not live on the campus or eat at any of the school's dining halls. But they gave him a job operating a freight elevator in the state office building to pay his way. No black colleges had offered him a scholarship of any kind.

On May 25, 1935, at the National Intercollegiate track meet, Owens had what is still considered the most spectacular day in track and field history. He set world records in the 220-yard dash, 220-yard low hurdles, and long jump, and tied the record for the 100-yard dash. He also won two other races. The most amazing part of his feat was that he did it all within 45 minutes.

But Jesse was not unbeatable. He lost some sprints that year, including losses to 1932 Olympic medalist Ralph Metcalfe. Jesse won everything he entered at the Big 10 track meet

Jesse Owens set an Olympic record in the long jump in 1936, defeating the German favorite. The crowd cheered him, but dictator Adolf Hitler refused to congratulate any of the black winners.

in 1936, breaking the world record for the 100-yard dash with a time of 9.3 seconds, before departing for the Olympics.

Olympic rules limited athletes to three individual events. Owens chose the 100- and 200-meter sprints and the long jump. Despite competition from Metcalfe and Mack Robinson (Jackie Robinson's brother), he went to Berlin as the favorite to win all three events.

Owens' exploits were well known to the German people. Despite Hitler's harangues about white superiority, they shed their political feelings and eagerly mobbed Owens on his arrival. They besieged him for autographs and cheered his every move on the field. But not Hitler. As the Games began, Hitler had the winners brought to his box to congratulate them—until two black Americans, Cornelius Johnson and David Albritton, finished first and second in the high jump. Hitler then stopped inviting the winners to meet him.

Owens did not disappoint his fans. On August 3, the second day of the Games, he won the 100-meter race by a yard over Ralph Metcalfe. The next day he won his second gold medal with an Olympic record long jump of 26' 5 $1/2$", beating the blond German hopeful, Luz Long, who openly congratulated him while the crowd cheered and Hitler watched in silence.

A light rain fell on the morning of Wednesday, August 5, as Owens and Mack Robinson qualified for that afternoon's 200-meter finals. Owens won his third gold, edging Robinson by less than a half second. In his 12 qualifying or final efforts, Owens had tied or broken four world records and nine Olympic marks. No athlete had won three individual golds since 1900.

Owens' work was done. Or so he thought.

The American 400-meter relay team included two Jewish runners, Marty Glickman and Sam Stoller. Although Glickman and Stoller had qualified for the team along with Mack Robinson, team officials cut all three at the last minute and added Owens, Ralph Metcalfe, and Frank Wykoff in their place.

The change touched off speculation that the two Jews had been denied a chance to compete in order to appease Hitler. Rumors spread that Owens had selfishly asked to be on the team so that he might win a fourth gold. The speculation about Hitler may have been true, but the rumors were not. In a team meeting, Owens pleaded with the coaches to let the others run. His request was denied, and Owens reluctantly ran the first leg of the relay, which the Americans won easily in record time.

The first American—and third athlete—to win four gold medals at one Olympics, Owens returned home to a ticker tape parade in New York City. He turned professional to cash in on his fame. But the world of track and field was strictly amateur at that time.

He had been born 50 years too soon to enjoy million-dollar prizes and endorsements. The best he could do was a series of exhibitions and novelty races. He toured with fellow Olympian Helen Stephens, winner of two golds in Berlin, and was matched against racehorses, dogs, and motorcyclists. Most of the business ventures he was involved in failed. He made speaking appearances for various corporations and wrote two books.

Owens died in 1980. Four years later a street in Berlin was named for him.

2

RUNNING FOR THEIR LIVES

From the time the earliest humans stood upright and walked, they have been running, jumping, and throwing things. But these were not done for fun and games; they did these things literally to save their lives.

Before people had tools to use for farming and hunting, they lived on berries and plants. When attacked by animals bigger and stronger than they were, their only defenses were to run away or pick up a rock and throw it. Faced with a human enemy who wanted something he had, early humans could only run or fight with their hands. "Survival goes to the swiftest" was more than a motto; it was a fact of life.

During the Stone Age, and later the Bronze and Iron Ages, men used weapons like spears, flat stones, and slings, and became hunters for meat. The best meat and the highest honors in a tribe or village went to those who could run the fastest in pursuit of game, and throw a javelin (a lightweight spear) or hurl a flat stone (discus) the farthest to bring down a deer or other fleet-footed animal.

Men continued to hunt even after they had the tools and know-how to raise crops. They settled down in larger communities. But now, in addition to defending hunting territories from attackers, they had to defend their crops and property, as well as their families, from invaders. Warriors who excelled at the skills now associated

Activities similar to today's track and field events were depicted in ancient tomb paintings as everyday skills needed in hunting and combat.

with track and field events became celebrated. Prizes and positions of leadership were bestowed upon them.

The pedestals upon which society now places sports heroes are no different from the practice of millions of years ago. Ancient hieroglyphics and pictographs extolled their accomplishments just as this book tells of the heroic achievements of Jesse Owens, Jim Thorpe, Babe Didrikson, and Carl Lewis.

Jealousy and competitive instincts have always been part of human nature. It was inevitable that the glory and honors won by the best hunters and warriors would spur other men to vie for those prizes. Contrary to some theories, modern track and field sports did not grow out of children's games. It was the other way around. The importance of running and throwing to survival led to the training of young boys in those skills. Inspired by the fireside tales told by their fathers, boys made their own weapons and practiced throwing them. Among some tribes, a dispute over hunting rights or farmland might be settled by a race or other kind of contest instead of a fight to the death.

Ancient peoples worshipped many gods. The success of vital crops depended on rainfall and sunlight at the right times, which were beyond the control of humans. So they devised rituals that might please the sun and moon and weather gods. While they did not think of it that way, they hoped that the gods were sports fans, and conducted track meets and ball games to gain the favor of the invisible but all-powerful deities.

These practices were common throughout Africa and the area that is now Europe, and

among the Indian tribes of North and South America. Illustrations of many kinds of sports appear on the walls of Egyptian tombs dating back thousands of years. The Apache Indians relied on relay races of young boys, accompanied by elaborate dances and other religious rituals, to please their gods.

The holding of festivals to honor ancestral heroes or great victories in battle has been a universal custom for millennia. Contests of physical strength and skill often lasted for several days, followed by ceremonies and feasts. Wars were interrupted for the funeral of a slain chief, and did not resume until appropriate field games took place to commemorate the departed leader. These events drew throngs of spectators who cheered outstanding performances, placed bets and loudly urged on

Runners were used as messengers carrying news from battle-fields, as portrayed on this 2,500-year-old Grecian urn.

their favorites, and jeered at contestants who fell or threw poorly. The sounds and reactions of those early fans were the same as those heard in any modern stadium today.

The Greeks carried these games to the highest level of organization in the ancient world. Distance races, discus and spear throwing, and broad jumping were on the program, along with wrestling, archery, and chariot races. Rich patrons of the games put up prize money. The word athlete is a Greek word meaning to contend for a prize.

The mild year-round climate around the Mediterranean Sea enabled hundreds of cities throughout the Greek-controlled region to hold festivals, providing full-time athletes a circuit to travel. A few festivals emerged as the largest and most prestigious. Gradually, the meet at Olympia, a remote spot near the sea and far removed from Athens, Sparta, or other big cities, became the "Super Bowl" equivalent of Greek games. Held every four years as a tribute to Zeus, the mightiest of the gods, the games in the valley of Olympia evolved into the Olympic Games.

Nobody knows who started them or when, or exactly what kinds of races and other contests took place. Olympia had been a religious shrine to Zeus for hundreds of years before the first written records appeared in the form of the name of a winner of a 200-meter race in 776 B.C. Gradually races of greater lengths— including one run in full battle armor—and other non-track events were added to the program.

Although no monetary prizes were awarded at Olympia, a win there gave an athlete's career a big boost, enabling him to draw invitations from other major meets around the circuit. The practice of an amateur athlete using a big win for a springboard to a career as a full-time professional thus began thousands of years before sneaker and cereal endorsements and TV commercials.

The Olympic Games, mixed with religious ceremonies, remained essentially the same for a thousand years. The crowds grew until the Olympics became the highlight of the athletic calendar. The tiny valley lacked any facilities to house and feed the multitudes who braved the summer heat and inconvenience for the five-day Games. Eventually the officials built a stadium and other structures.

The chariot race, with highly decorated two-wheeled vehicles pulled by four horses, was the most spectacular event. But the athletes who excelled at the pentathlon earned the most lasting praise from the poets and sculptors. The pentathlon combined five tests of skill and strength: throwing the discus, a round, flat stone; throwing a six-foot-long javelin or spear; the standing broad jump; a 200-meter race; and a wrestling match.

Religious ceremonies always followed the games. Everybody enjoyed a good meal on the last day when 100 oxen were slain for Zeus and roasted for the athletes and spectators.

The Olympic Games were all-male. Women were not allowed to compete or attend. The athletes competed nude, but that was not the reason women were banned. (Once, the mother of an athlete sneaked in disguised as a trainer to watch her son compete. When he won, she got so excited, she was discovered. Thereafter,

This panorama of games played by Greeks includes chariot races, which were the highlight of the original Olympic Games almost 3,000 years ago.

trainers had to leave their clothes at the entrance, too.) In the Greek world of 2,500 years ago, all matters of importance were attended to exclusively by the men. Only men were trained in the skills used in battle, the same skills involved in the competitions.

Some independent women held their own games at Olympia at other times, consisting mostly of footraces, wrestling, and chariot races. Gradually, games at other locations included races for women, but they were never allowed to compete in the original Olympic Games.

The Roman Empire conquered Greece and the rest of the known world around the Mediterranean, but the combination of religious rites and athletic games continued at Olympia. The Romans sponsored games of their own there. But the discomforts and remote location of Olympia led to its decline. Games in the cities offered attractive prizes and convenient facilities, and drew larger crowds.

As the influence of Christianity spread, Roman emperors tried to extinguish other religious practices. Since the worship of Zeus had always been an integral part of the event at Olympia, the Olympic Games lost their meaning as the Greek gods declined in importance. The Olympic Games disappeared in the fifth century. One hundred years later, two earthquakes destroyed whatever buildings remained.

3 LET THE GAMES BEGIN

The emphasis on physical fitness to prepare men for combat continued in some countries for centuries. Englishmen in the 19th century boasted that their military victories had been won because of their soldiers' training on prep school playing fields.

Nationalism and ethnic pride combined with the competitive instinct to foster athletic matches, which offered a peaceful form of combat to win bragging rights as well as prizes. For some groups, athletics were the only way they could demonstrate some kind of superiority without fearing for their safety. They didn't need any equipment—not even shoes—to run.

For the slaves in America, athletics were often their only form of recreation. Frederick Douglass wrote of slaves spending their holidays "in sports, ballplaying, wrestling, boxing, foot racing." Slave children delighted in being able to outrun and outjump the sons and daughters of their masters. Indian tribes, who had depended on speed and endurance for survival, took pride in competing against blacks and whites.

The 19th-century American penchant for organizing and promoting led inevitably to organized running and walking races for cash prizes. Promoters drew crowds by carefully inviting a mix of entries from many ethnic groups. In the North blacks freely entered races against Irish, English, and Indian runners.

In a dramatic finish to the marathon at the 1908 Olympics in London, Dorando Pietri of Italy staggered into the stadium first, then ran the wrong way before collapsing from exhaustion. Officials kindly but illegally dragged him across the finish line.

Following the Civil War, new ideas and methods of training emerged. Social clubs and ethnic groups sought out the best athletes to represent them, and sponsored them by providing training facilities, coaches, and living expenses. Such clubs were usually open to "white gentlemen" only. As they gradually took over the running of track meets, they refused to recognize winners and possible records set outside their domain.

The New York Athletic Club was a pioneer in this movement. Organized in 1866, it held its first meet five years later. The Amateur Athletic Union was formed in 1888 and eventually set the rules and standards for track and field events in the United States. Other clubs held their own meets. Interest sifted down to the public schools, resulting in the formation of the Public Schools Athletic League in New York City.

Track meets began at the college level in 1873. At first the long distance races were the most popular. College activity led to the National Collegiate Athletic Association (NCAA) and eventually to organized regional and national meets.

Integrated colleges in the North welcomed black track stars. In the South, black colleges held their own competitions. National games became integrated in 1895.

The biggest boost for track and field came from a tiny Frenchman who neither ran nor jumped. Pierre de Coubertin almost single-handedly revived the Olympic Games 1,500 years after they had ceased. Born in Paris in 1863, the 5' 3" de Coubertin was no athlete. But in his travels to England and America he was impressed by the athletic activities he saw. In France, sports and outdoor games were not considered important for students. He returned home determined to promote athletics in French schools.

During the 1880s German archaeologists had spent six years uncovering the remains of the buildings at Olympia. De Coubertin visited the digs and was struck with the thought: why not hold such games today? The 19th century had been scarred by more wars than peacetime, both in America and Europe. He envisioned peaceful gatherings of athletes from all over the world, competing with their arms and legs instead of cannons and bayonets.

De Coubertin first suggested the idea in 1892. Nobody was interested. Two years later, at an international athletic conference, he brought it up again. This time he had a more receptive audience. They considered renewing the ancient games at their original site, Olympia. But the ruins in the remote spit of land were too far gone to reconstruct, so they chose the city of Athens instead. The Greek government had no money to build a stadium, so a wealthy Greek merchant put up the entire cost of restoring a 2,000-year-old stadium in the city. The games were scheduled for 1896.

Ten track and field men, half of whom paid their own way, formed the entire United States delegation. One of them, James B. Connolly, a Harvard student, won the first gold medal, in the triple jump. Another, Bob Garrett from Maryland, won the shot put. While in Athens he picked up the five-pound discus one day and decided to enter that event, too. He won a second gold, and added two silver medals before the Games were over.

Americans won nine of the 12 track and field events. Enthusiastic Greek crowds filled the stadium and the embankments around it.

The Olympic Games did not grow from their auspicious debut. Officials made the mistake of awarding the 1900 Games to Paris, where the French remained indifferent to sports. No tracks or fields had been properly prepared. Even though admission was free, few people came to watch the five days of events.

Four years later, in St. Louis, Missouri, they fared little better. Few Europeans made the long journey; England and France did not even bother to send a single athlete. The Americans' 21 gold medals in 22 events meant little. Crowds were small.

Disappointed and fearful that the Games would fade away before the 1908 event scheduled for London, de Coubertin returned to the scene of his inaugural success, Athens. He proposed adding an Athenian meet every four years between Olympics. The Greeks were still enthused and, in 1906, huge crowds turned out for the Games. For the first time, the United States organized an official team that traveled and trained together, financed by public contributions. A record number of athletes and countries participated. The 35-man American team won 11 of the 19 track and field events. But political unrest in Greece scuttled the 1910 Games, and the so-called "unofficial Olympics" was never held again.

The Olympic Games gained more solid footing when 25 nations sent representatives to Stockholm in 1912. The Games were not held in 1916 during World War I, and were again interrupted in the 1940s during World

Dorando Pietri and 1908 marathon winner John Hayes staged a series of races in the United States. Here they are about to start a marathon in New York City.

War II, but they have been held every four years since 1948. Some nations have boycotted the Games from time to time; the United States stayed away from the 1980 Games in Moscow to protest the Soviet invasion of Afghanistan. Four years later, the Soviets retaliated by staying away from Los Angeles.

In 1896 Pierre de Coubertin established the Olympic Creed when he said, "The important thing in the Olympic Games is not winning but taking part. The essential thing in life is not conquering but fighting well."

Despite the legend of Pheidippides and his fatal run from the Battle of Marathon, the marathon race was not included in the ancient list of games held at Olympia.

Pierre de Coubertin and French historian Michel Breal first proposed the event to the Greek hosts of the 1896 Games. The connection with Greek history proved irresistible to the organizers. They were overjoyed when Spirido Loues, a Greek shepherd from a small village, won it, with two fellow Greeks finishing second and third.

The popularity of the race was matched by the peculiarities that accompanied it for the next 12 years. In 1900 the course wound through the streets of Paris. An American, Arthur Newton, led the field from the midway

Dan Flanagan won the hammer throw and two other events at the 1900 Olympics in Paris.

point. But when he arrived near the finish line inside the stadium, he found a French baker there ahead of him. The Frenchman was declared the winner, even though he had apparently never passed Newton on the way.

In St. Louis in 1904, one runner, Fred Lorz, got tired and climbed into an automobile that chugged alongside the runners. Lorz got out after riding for several miles and resumed running. He finished first, but was disqualified before the medals were handed out.

In the London marathon of 1908, a small Italian candy maker, Dorando Pietri, arrived first at the stadium where the finish line awaited. But he was so exhausted, he began running in the wrong direction, then collapsed on the track. The next to enter the scene was an American department store clerk, John Hayes. British officials did not want to see the American win. They picked up Dorando and dragged him across the finish line ahead of Hayes. The Americans cried foul. Their protest was upheld, and Hayes was declared the winner.

Dorando Pietri and John Hayes turned professional and ran against each other for prize money in three marathons in New York. Pietri won two and a French runner won the third. Since then, annual marathons have become popular in many American cities, drawing thousands of entrants from all over the world.

Martin Sheridan took gold medals in the discus in 1904, 1906, and 1908.

4   THE EARLY STARS

The evolution of people over the past 100 years resulted in taller and stronger men and women who eclipsed record performances that once awed the world.

The title of "The World's Fastest Human" belonged to Charlie Paddock in the 1920s. Born in Gainesville, Texas in 1900, Paddock was a puny infant. He weighed only 7 1/2 pounds when he was seven months old. His family moved to California for the healthier climate in 1907.

Charlie discovered that he could run faster than other kids, and he became unbeatable in short sprints. In his twenties, he set records for 100-yard and 200-yard dashes. He brought cheers from crowds with his trademark flying finish, leaping through the air as he neared the finish line and breaking the tape with his chest in midair.

But Paddock ran afoul of the rules of amateur athletics in the 1920s. Anyone earning money doing anything connected with track and field came under suspicion. The rules were so strict that athletes could lose their amateur standing and become ineligible to compete if they were paid for coaching, or if their friends and neighbors were too generous in raising prize money for them. In Paddock's case, he had written newspaper articles about running and appeared in a movie, so he was suspended from competing in amateur meets. The suspensions were lifted

Charlie Paddock leaps through the air at the finish line in one of his record-breaking 100-yard sprints. Paddock was called "The World's Fastest Human" in the 1920s.

for the Olympic Games. Paddock won a total of two gold and two silver medals in three Olympics. A newspaper executive when he enlisted in the Marines in World War II, Paddock was killed in a military plane crash in Alaska in 1943.

Some athletes captured the hearts of fans by overcoming physical handicaps to become track stars. Glenn Cunningham recovered from an accident that left him unable to walk, and became the world's fastest miler.

Born August 4, 1909, in Atlanta, Kansas, Glenn and his older brother, Floyd, went to a one-room schoolhouse. When Glenn was six, they had the chore of starting the fire in the school's stove on cold winter mornings. One day someone accidentally filled the kerosene can with gasoline. When the boys poured the gasoline into the stove, it exploded. Floyd was killed; Glenn was so badly burned his parents feared he would never walk again.

For several years Glenn got around on crutches. Then he made a strange discovery: his legs hurt when he tried to walk, but they did not hurt when he ran. So he began to run everywhere, and built up enough stamina to set a world record of 4:04.4 for the mile in 1938. But the race was not part of a sanctioned meet, so his time was not recognized by the governors of track and field at the time. Cunningham won 22 mile races at major track meets in the 1930s, but he never won an Olympic gold. Later, four minutes became a slow time for the mile.

Betty Robinson was a 16-year-old high school student in Riverdale, Illinois, in 1928. One day a coach saw her running for a bus, and thought she was fast enough to compete in track meets. Betty ran in only three races before she found herself on the women's Olympic team headed for Amsterdam. It was the first time a track event for women had been added to the Games, and Betty Robinson won the inaugural 100-meter sprint.

Three years after her triumph, Robinson was severely injured in an airplane crash. It took her two years to recover; when her broken leg healed, it left her unable to fully bend her knee. Unable to crouch for the start of a sprint, she ran as a member of the U.S. 400-meter relay team in 1936, and picked up a second gold medal.

Early record setters were limited by the equipment of the time. Using a bamboo pole, pole vaulter Cornelius Warmerdam was the first to top 15 feet, reaching that height on April 13, 1940. The cancellation of the Olympics in 1940 and 1944 cost him chances to win gold medals. He retired before the 1948 Games and became a track and basketball coach at Fresno State University. Later, the use of aluminum poles helped vaulters to pass his record.

Jim Thorpe was considered the greatest American athlete of the first half of the 20th century. Part French, Irish, and Sac and Fox Indian, Thorpe earned the tribal name of Bright Path. As a youth in Oklahoma, he chased wild ponies on foot, caught them, and climbed on their backs. He starred in football and track at Carlisle College, a school for Indians in Pennsylvania. In one track meet, he and six teammates took on a 48-man team from Lafayette. Thorpe won six events in his team's 71–41 win.

Jim Thorpe may be the greatest athlete in American history. After winning golds in the pentathlon and decathlon in 1912, he played professional football and major league baseball.

It seemed as if Paavo Nurmi, "The Flying Finn," could run all day without tiring. He won four golds in the 1924 Olympics, then toured the United States, winning all but one race.

Thorpe played professional football and major league baseball, but he gained his greatest fame as a track star. In the 1912 Olympics in Stockholm, he won both the pentathlon and decathlon, the two most demanding events of the Games. He came home to a hero's reception—a parade in New York City, after which he said, "I heard people yelling my name, and I couldn't realize how one fellow could have so many friends."

But there were rain clouds forming over Thorpe's parade. He had begun his baseball career by playing in the minor leagues in 1909. The Amateur Athletic Union, which ruled the Games at the time, frowned on amateurs earning money from playing any sport, even if it was not an Olympic event. They forced Thorpe to give back his two gold medals and other trophies he had won since 1909.

In 1983, 30 years after Thorpe died, the medals he won were returned to his children.

A dozen years after Jim Thorpe's glorious triumph, the world acclaimed a new track hero, Paavo Nurmi, "The Flying Finn." Inspired by a countryman's three long distance victories in the 1912 Olympics, the 15-year-old Nurmi dreamed of following in his track steps. He trained by running behind trolley cars for miles through the city and out into the countryside. Nurmi developed a steady, almost mechanical pace that made him look like a robot. He ignored the others in a race and ran against the watch on his wrist, gradually improving his time for each segment of a race.

In the 1920 Olympics at Antwerp, Belgium, Nurmi won two golds and a silver, but that was just the beginning for the 23-year-old mechanical man. He kept pushing his endurance a little more with each race during the next four years, regularly shaving seconds off world records for long-distance and cross-country events.

Nurmi arrived at the 1924 Games in Paris in peak condition. In one afternoon he won both the 1,500- meter and 5,000- meter races in Olympic record times. Two days later, in heat that caused more than half the field to drop out along the way, Nurmi won the cross-country race with ease. The other 14 who finished collapsed in exhaustion. But Nurmi was so fresh, the next day he ran as part of Finland's winning 3,000-meter team and earned his fourth gold medal.

The world marveled at the Flying Finn's superhuman endurance. Like a machine that never wore down, he ran with no expression on his face and no signs of ever tiring. After a race he had very little to say to the press, but it was not from being weary. He was simply a man of few words.

In the winter of 1925 Nurmi toured the United States, drawing huge crowds to indoor meets. Despite a grueling travel schedule, he won every race except a half-mile event, which was not his usual distance. Near the end of the tour he became the first to run the two-mile distance in under nine minutes.

At the athletically advanced age of 31, Nurmi won a gold and two silvers at the 1928 Olympics.

5   WOMEN WHO STARRED

Although small groups of women held their own competitions in ancient Olympia, athletics remained a man's world for thousands of years. There were no women's track events in the Olympics until 1928, and then only a few. Gradually, events for women expanded to include almost all the same ones as for men.

But a late start did not prevent women from achieving outstanding performances in track and field. In fact, the most versatile athlete in American history was a woman.

Mildred Didrikson was born on June 26, 1914, in Port Arthur, Texas, to Norwegian immigrant parents. As a teenager playing softball, she hit home runs as far and as often as Babe Ruth, then at the height of his power and fame. Mildred's friends started calling her Babe, and the name stuck.

Babe trained with homemade weights made from broom handles and old flat irons. She set up gymnastics equipment in her backyard. When she was 18 she went to work as a typist for an insurance company in Dallas. The company sponsored athletic teams, but they had no other employees who could run and jump and throw like Babe. So they sent her as their one-person track team to represent them at the 1932 Amateur Athletic Union national championships. Other teams had dozens of athletes.

Babe won five events, setting world records in the javelin throw and 60-meter hurdles, and tied

Mildred "Babe" Didrikson Zaharias was the greatest woman athlete of all time. Here she runs a hurdles race in a 1932 team track meet in which she beat all the other teams single-handedly.

for high jump honors. Altogether Babe scored 30 points to win the team championship all by herself. Babe went from there to the Olympics in Los Angeles, where she won the javelin throw with an Olympic record, and set a world mark of 11.7 seconds in the 80-meter hurdles.

Babe Didrikson married a professional wrestler, George Zaharias, and became a professional baseball and basketball player, golfer, and billiards expert. She conquered everything she took on except the cancer that killed her in 1956.

Babe Zaharias was a career athlete, but the woman who starred at the 1948 Olympics was a 30-year-old housewife from Holland. Fanny Blankers-Koen held world records in sprints and jumping, but the cancellation of the 1940 and 1944 Games delayed her chances to go for the gold until she was past the prime age for athletes. Nevertheless, she won four gold medals, in sprints, hurdles, and relay races, becoming the first woman to take home four golds from one Olympics. Had she been allowed to enter the long jump, she probably would have won five.

There have been other women athletes who were versatile and talented, but they rarely received much publicity. One was Helen Stephens, born in Fulton, Missouri, in 1918. One day on the high school playground during phys ed class, Helen ran a 50-yard dash. A teacher who timed her could not believe that she had tied the world record of 5.8 seconds. A coach began working with her and, at 17, she went to the national AAU indoor meet, where she tied the world record in the 50-meter sprint and won the shot put and standing

Helen Stephens never lost a race. After winning four golds in the 1936 Olympics, she retired at age 19. Here she relaxes with Jesse Owens during the Games in Berlin.

broad jump. In college she made the bowling, basketball, fencing, and swimming teams.

At the 1936 Olympics in Berlin, the 6' 18-year-old won the 100-meter dash in a world record 11.5 seconds, and gained a second gold medal as part of the 400-meter relay team. Stephens retired at 19 without ever losing a race. Then she toured with Jesse Owens in a series of exhibition races. She played professional softball and basketball, and joined the Marines in World War II. When she was in her sixties, Stephens took part in the Senior Olympics for seven years and never lost a race.

Irena Szewinska won seven medals in five different events in four Olympics, beginning in 1964. After 10 years of specializing in short sprints and the long jump, the native of Leningrad switched to the longer 400-meter distance and immediately became the first woman to break 50 seconds. In 1976 at Montreal, the 30-year-old took on her 18-year-old rival, Christina Brehmer, and left her trailing by 10 meters at the finish line.

As training equipment and college programs for women improved, more women went out for track. Alice Coachman, AAU champion high jumper for 10 years, became the first black woman to win a gold at the London Games in 1948. But the success and acclaim achieved by Wilma Rudolph inspired other black women to become interested in the sport.

The 20th of 22 children, Wilma weighed only $4^1/2$ pounds when she was born in St. Bethlehem, Tennessee, in 1940. Weakened by early bouts of polio, double pneumonia, and scarlet fever, she wore a brace on her leg until she was 12. Every day her mother and brothers and sisters took turns massaging her legs. By the time she was in high school, Wilma stood 5'11" and was starring in basketball and track. She made the Olympic team when she was 16, won a bronze medal in Australia in a relay, and arrived home in time to play in a school basketball game.

In 1960 Rudolph led a powerful Tennessee State Tigerbelles team to the Olympics in Rome. Blessed with the ability to sleep anytime and anywhere, she took a nap before her semifinal heat in the 100-meter race, went on to win the finals, and took two other gold medals. She set a world record of 22.9 seconds in the 200-meter sprint.

Rudolph established a foundation to sponsor competition and help young athletes obtain better training programs and equipment.

Florence Griffith-Joyner earned more publicity from her colorful running suits, long, brightly colored fingernails, and free spirit than from her running. Born Delorez Florence Griffith in 1959 in the Watts section of Los

Angeles, she was outrunning everybody in the neighborhood by the time she was seven. Her speed helped her land a scholarship at UCLA.

Griffith-Joyner rarely won a major race and had to settle for a silver medal at the 1984 games in Los Angeles. Determined to win in 1988, she embarked on a serious training program of weight lifting, long-distance running, and studying videotapes of male sprint champions. Her dedication paid off with gold medals and record times in the 100- and 200-meters, and a third gold and a silver in relays. Flo-Jo then retired and became a fashion designer.

Jackie Joyner added to the achievements being turned in by black women. Born in East St. Louis, Illinois, in 1960, Jackie starred at UCLA in the long jump and pentathlon.

Olympic officials added the seven-event heptathlon to the Games in 1984; Joyner finished second. After marrying her coach, Bob Kersee, in 1986, she won world championships and set records in the long jump and heptathlon in 1987. Then, as Jackie Joyner-Kersee, she won the next two Olympic heptathlons.

Crippled by polio, Wilma Rudolph recovered and went on to win three gold medals at the 1960 Olympics in Rome. Here she leads the U.S. team to a victory in a Moscow meet.

6 POSTWAR HEROES

The stepped-up emphasis on physical fitness caused by America's involvement in World War II continued after the war ended in 1945. Aided by better nutrition and training, and more knowledge about how muscles work, athletes grew bigger and stronger than ever. Track records fell like straw huts in a hurricane, a phenomenon that has continued to the present.

The biggest hero returning from the first postwar Games in London in 1948 was Bob Mathias. The youngest ever to win a men's track and field gold medal, the 17-year-old Mathias starred in football, basketball, and track at his Tulare, California, high school. After winning the two-day decathlon, which did not end until 10:35 on the dark and rainy night of the second day, Mathias went to Stanford, where he played football. By 1952 he had grown to 6' 3" and 205 pounds.

In 1952 at Helsinki, Mathias became the only person to win the decathlon twice, this time with a record 7,887 points, 900 more than the runner-up. Bob Mathias later became a congressman and the director of the Olympic training center in Colorado Springs.

On May 6, 1954, a British medical student named Roger Bannister became the first to run a mile in under four minutes. His record time of 3:59.4 lasted only six weeks; on June 21 John Landy of Australia lowered it to 3:58. In the next

A star high school athlete from California, Bob Mathias became the only person to win the grueling decathlon event twice in Olympic history.

few years, eight other runners broke the four-minute mark.

Jim Ryun, born in 1947 in Wichita, Kansas, was the first high school student to break the four-minute mile. As a freshman at the University of Kansas, Ryun ran a record 3:55.3 mile, and lowered it to 3:51.1 in 1967. He also held world records in the 880-yard and 1,500-meter distances. Illness and the high altitude in Mexico City hindered him in the 1968 Olympics; he finished second in the 1,500 meters. In 1972 at the Munich Games he fell at the start of the race. Ryun ran in professional meets in the 1970s.

Pole vault records also tumbled, as Bob Richards topped 15 feet 126 times from 1947 to 1957. Using an aluminum pole instead of

On May 6, 1954, Roger Bannister became the first to run a mile in under four minutes. Here he crosses the finish line ahead of John Landy in the first race in which two runners broke the four-minute mark.

an old-style bamboo pole, Richards won golds in 1952 and '56 as the "Vaulting Vicar," having been ordained a minister in 1948. Richards retired in 1957, leaving him free to accept payment for his face appearing on cereal boxes and advertisements.

YMCA, company-sponsored, and church track teams gave way to college and club teams. More national and international games, such as the Goodwill and Pan Am meets, appeared on the schedule. Women's participation sky-rocketed. But there were still no coordinated national training programs in the United States. That was left to the individual clubs and schools, many of which remained restricted to whites only in the 1950s.

Black athletes relied on college programs in the North, and black colleges in the South. As facilities and coaching improved, the United States sent large, strong track teams, invigo-rated by black male and female athletes, to international meets.

Rafer Johnson, a football, baseball, and basketball star in high school in California, was a sprinter and long jumper. After winning a silver in 1956, Johnson won the honor of carrying the American flag in the 1960 opening ceremonies, and capped it by winning a gold in the decathlon. In 1984 Johnson lit the torch to commence the Games in Los Angeles.

Ralph Boston, who topped Jesse Owens' long jump record in 1960, went on to lengthen the record four more times.

Bob Hayes became the next to carry the tag of "World's Fastest Human." Born in Jacksonville, Florida, in 1942, Hayes was the first to run 100 yards in 9.1 seconds, and 60

Rafer Johnson puts the shot in one of the 10 events of the demanding decathlon he won in the 1960 Olympics.

"Bullet" Bob Hayes, Florida A & M sophomore, sprints to the tape in 9.2 seconds to tie the world record in the 100-yard dash in 1962. Hayes later starred for the Dallas Cowboys.

yards in under 6 seconds. In Tokyo in 1964 he electrified the spectators by winning the short 100-meter sprint by an incredible 7 feet over his nearest competitor. Running the last leg of the 400-meter relay, he brought the crowd to its feet by outrunning the leader by 7 yards in 9 seconds to bring the American team the gold.

Hayes looked awkward when he ran. One coach described him as running "like he was pounding grapes into wine." Hayes liked to say of himself, "I'm just a country boy goin' to the city with taps on my tennis shoes."

Hayes later played 12 years as a wide receiver for the Dallas Cowboys.

Thirteen-year-old Harrison Dillard watched a parade for Jesse Owens in Cleveland in 1936, and vowed that some day he would come home a hero, too. Nicknamed "Bones" because he weighed only 150 pounds, Dillard received his first running shoes from Owens. He was unbeaten in 82 hurdles races in 1947–48, and won a sprint gold in 1948 and a gold in hurdles in 1952.

These are a few of the athletes who launched the postwar assault on the record books and brought growing attention to the world of track and field.

7 RECORD SETTERS

Although records for time and distance in track and field events last about as long as a box of brownies at a boys' camp, some record-setting performances will never be forgotten. And at least one will never be equaled.

In the Paris Olympics of 1900, Alvin C. Kraenzlein won individual gold medals in the 60-meter dash, 110- and 220-meter hurdles, and the long jump. A Wisconsin native, Kraenzlein was the first to clear the hurdles with one leg straight out and the other tucked under him. At one time he held world records in six events. All have since been broken, except for his four individual gold medals in one Olympics. Soon after that, the rules were changed, limiting contestants to three individual events. Athletes like Jesse Owens could win a fourth only as part of a relay team.

Edwin Moses was an engineering and physics student at Morehouse College in Atlanta before he was a track star. Almost a straight-A student, Moses ran the 110-meter high hurdles and 400-meter dash. But he regretted taking time from his studies to train.

A coach urged him to try the 400-meter hurdles and aim for the 1976 Olympics in Montreal. He ran only one race at that distance before the Olympics, then ran away from the field in a world record 47.63 seconds to win the gold. As he crossed the finish line, his nearest

Carl Lewis sticks out his tongue as he flies through the air in the long jump at the 1984 Olympics in Los Angeles. Lewis won the same four events that Jesse Owens had won in 1936.

competitor was an incredible 8 meters back, a record margin for that event.

The next year Moses began a 107-race winning streak that covered races in 22 countries and lasted almost 10 years. He kept whittling his time until it reached 47.02 seconds, and at one time he owned the nine fastest times for the event in the record books.

The high altitude in Mexico City in 1968 bothered some athletes, but it didn't stop Bob Beamon from making history. A long jump specialist born in Jamaica, New York, in 1946, the 21-year-old Beamon had lost only once in 23 meets that year, representing the University of Texas-El Paso. But at the Olympics he was up against the three medal winners from 1964, including the veteran Ralph Boston, the first to jump 27 feet, and the first to top Jesse Owens' 1936 record after 24 years.

Beamon had set indoor records in the long jump of just over 27 feet that winter. While warming up for the event in Mexico City, he said to Ralph Boston, "I feel I can jump 28 feet today."

The other jumpers scraped checkmarks alongside the runway to help them maintain the proper stride on their approach. Beamon did not. In his qualifying jumps, Beamon twice fouled by landing on his takeoff foot past the launching board. With one last chance to qualify, he heeded some advice from his opponent, Boston, and took off before he reached the board.

Rain clouds gathered as Beamon waited his turn in the finals. At 3:36 P.M. his number, 254, was called. He started down the 130-foot runway. His right foot pushed off the takeoff

board. He soared through the air, oblivious to the crowd and the noise around him, and seemed to float forever. When he hit the sand, he had the feeling that he had beaten his own record, maybe even gone to 27' 6".

His distance did not show up on the judges' optical equipment, which had a range of 28 feet. They found a tape and measured the distance. Beamon had passed not only 28 feet but 29 as well. They measured again: 29' 2^1/2". He had beaten the world record by an amazing two feet.

It began to rain, but Bob Beamon never felt it. He turned numb and his legs collapsed when he realized what he had accomplished.

Robert Beamon digs his feet into the sand pit after a record-shattering long jump of 29' 2^1/2" in the 1968 Olympics in Mexico City.

In 1992 an American Olympic track coach called Carl Lewis "the greatest athlete I have ever seen." Born in Birmingham, Alabama, in 1961, Lewis grew up in Willingboro, New Jersey. When he was 15, he really "grew up," adding 2 $1/2$ inches in height so fast he had to walk on crutches for a month until his body could adjust.

Both of his parents were track coaches. They started a backyard track club for their three sons and a daughter. After his spurt of growth, Carl concentrated on the 100-meter dash and the long jump, first at the University of Houston, then representing the Santa Monica Track Club in California. In 1984 he won four gold medals in the same events that Jesse Owens had won in 1936.

Lewis faced formidable rivals in both his specialties. His greatest track ambition was to beat Bob Beamon's long jump record. By the time he was 19 he was rated the world's best in the event, and would be undefeated in his next 65 meets spanning 10 $1/2$ years. Although he often leaped past 28 feet, he had never reached 29.

His closest competition was Mike Powell, a Philadelphia native two years younger than Lewis. But Powell always finished second, until the world championships in Tokyo in 1991. In the early rounds, Lewis actually leaped more than 29 feet, but the wind was too strong behind him and the jump did not count.

The crowd eagerly awaited the next round, anticipating that they might see the world record broken. They were not disappointed, but Carl Lewis was. For it was Mike Powell who soared 29' 4$1/2$", two inches farther than

Beamon's record that had stood for 23 years. Lewis responded with a leap of 29'1$\frac{1}{4}$", but it was not enough.

Lewis won his fourth straight long jump Olympic gold medal in 1996, but he retired without ever passing 29 feet again.

Throughout the 1980s Lewis and Ben Johnson vied for the honor of the "World's Fastest Human." Born in Jamaica in 1961, Johnson moved with his family to Toronto when he was 14. Six months older than Johnson, Lewis won their first encounter when he was 19. In the 1984 Olympic 100-meter dash, Lewis won and Johnson finished third. But by 1986 Johnson had begun to beat Lewis consistently.

In running style, they were opposites. Lewis was an awkward starter who turned on the afterburners near the finish line. He was once clocked running 28 miles an hour at the tape. Johnson, a more muscular youth, launched himself at the start with such a powerful thrust, he sometimes lost his balance.

At the 1987 world championships in Rome, Johnson made headlines by setting a world record of 9.83 seconds. Lewis also made headlines by voicing suspicions that Johnson was using prohibited drugs and steroids, a charge Johnson strongly denied. Leading up to the 1988 Olympics, Lewis won their only race after the Rome incident.

In 1987 Carl Lewis's father died. At the funeral, Lewis placed the gold medal he had won in the 100-meter race in 1984 into his father's lifeless hands. "I'll win another one," he assured his mother.

Hoping to become the first man to win the 100-meter sprint in two consecutive Olympics,

Canada's Ben Johnson raises his arm after winning the 100-meter dash at the 1988 Olympics in Seoul. Johnson was later disqualified for using steroids and Carl Lewis, right, was declared the winner.

Lewis could not overcome Johnson's explosive start. His Olympic record time of 9.92 seconds was like a freight train next to the Johnson express's world record 9.79.

Lewis was convinced that Johnson was still using steroids, but he said nothing. "I didn't have the medal to replace the one I had given (my father)," he wrote in his autobiography, *Inside Track*, "and that hurt. But I could still give something to my father by acting the way he had always wanted me to act, with class and dignity." He shook hands with Johnson without a word.

However, the routine testing for drugs that followed every event proved that Johnson had indeed been using steroids. At first he denied it, but later he admitted that he had been using the banned substances since 1981. Johnson was disqualified and Lewis declared the winner. Johnson's record time of 9.83 set in Rome was also thrown out by the International Track Federation, leaving Lewis's 9.86 seconds as evidence that he was the fastest man in the world—at least until the next super speedster came along.

8 MONEY AND DRUGS

By the 1970s, commercialism was no longer frowned upon in amateur track and field. After amassing a record 8,618 points in the 1976 Olympic decathlon, Bruce Jenner earned millions with his wife in commercials and personal appearances.

Gradually the distinction between amateurs and professionals disappeared. The International Amateur Athletic Federation became a misleading title for the sport's world governing body. Prize money became more the rule than the exception. Athletes setting world records won cash bonuses of $50,000. Runners wore corporate names and logos on their chests and backs when competing.

On March 9, 1997, Stacy Dragila won the women's pole vault at the world indoor championships in Paris. She went home to Idaho expecting a check for $25,000 in the mail. Like all contestants, she had worn a small bib that had her number on it. It also carried the name of the meet's primary sponsor. But during her event, her bib became folded and the sponsor's name was covered. The games' officials decided that this was grounds to disqualify her. They withheld the money until two months later, after she wrote a letter of apology.

In addition to the prize money at each meet, the Grand Prix, a circuit of four meets in Europe, offered a bonus of 44 pounds of gold bars to any athlete who remained unbeaten through the tour.

Canadian sprinter Donavan Bailey looks to his right for American runner Michael Johnson, who pulled up lame in their 150-meter race on June 1, 1997, to determine the world's fastest human. Bailey won the race as Johnson failed to finish.

Gone were the days when physical education teachers were considered professionals and were banned from competing, and a Jim Thorpe could lose his medals because he had once played minor league baseball. Or was the modern scene so different after all, considering that thousands of years ago, winners of the Greek games had received prizes, money, and privileges from friends and city governments. Throughout the 20th century, amateur athletes had been supported by wealthy patrons or their governments. Now they were openly subsidized by equipment manufacturers.

The use of bodybuilding drugs continued to plague track officials. Various forms of stimulants had been used by athletes long before steroids. Marathoners had sipped a mixture of brandy and strychnine during the race in 1904. Some trainers fed their runners raw eggs in sherry wine before a race.

But the growth of new drugs after World War II led to the banning of all stimulants and muscle builders. The Olympic Committee began mandatory testing in 1989, but that led to more problems. Testing methods failed to keep pace with the introduction of new drugs, and trainers found ways to beat the tests. Athletes questioned the reliability of the tests, and some went to court to overturn their suspensions.

Mary Slaney, America's top female distance runner, was suspended after allegedly failing the drug tests at the 1996 Olympics in Atlanta. She claimed that the tests failed to give accurate results when applied to women. A year later she was cleared by U.S. track authorities.

Michael Johnson in the starting block to begin a 400-meter race at a Swiss meet in 1996.

Overlapping national and international governing bodies complicated the matter. Some countries refused to go along with the four-year suspensions meted out by the IAAF, which tried to ease the situation by reducing suspensions to two years beginning in 1997.

Meanwhile, on the track the battle for the crown of the speediest human carried far more than bragging rights for the victor when Michael Johnson and Donovan Bailey ran a two-man race in Toronto on June 1, 1997. Each sprinter received $500,000 just for showing up; another $1 million awaited the winner.

Bailey had set a world record of 9.84 seconds in the 100-meter dash at Atlanta in 1996. Johnson had set the 200-meter record of 19.32 seconds while winning two golds. As a compromise, the promoters of the race settled on 150 meters, a distance not run in any major meets.

As the race neared, it became evident that the two runners genuinely disliked each other, swapping taunts and put-downs in the press. The race itself proved less exciting than the buildup; Bailey exploded out of the starting blocks and quickly led by a stride. Just past the halfway point, Johnson pulled up limping and dropped out. Bailey turned and derisively waved for Johnson to come on as he crossed the finish line.

At a meet in Paris, Johnson lost his first 400-meter race in eight years, but came back to win in the world championship in Athens. Interest in track and field was in the doldrums in the United States, but it remained high in Europe. Crowds of 70,000 turned out for the meet in Greece in the summer of 1997.

Runners from Kenya had dominated long-distance running since Kip Keino had set world records for 3,000 and 5,000 meters in 1965, and won the 1,500-meter gold in 1968. The tradition was picked up by his countryman, Daniel Komen, who became one of the wealthiest people in Kenya, where the annual per capita income was $280.

The 5' 7", 121-pound Komen trained as a child by running a total of 10 miles back and forth to school between the ages of 8 and 16.

At 19 he ran the second-fastest 5,000 meters in history. He earned $250,000 on the IAAF circuit in 1996, and even more under a Nike sponsorship in 1997. Competing sneaker companies dangled a $1 million prize if their sponsored runner broke a long distance record, like running two miles in under 8 minutes. Komen held the world record of 7:20.67 for 3,000 meters, a distance about 240 yards short of 2 miles.

The controversies over drugs and drug testing, rules and jurisdictions, and the commercialism of the sport deflected attention from what participating in track and field was all about: the long, arduous, sometimes lonely, sometimes joyful life of the would-be champion. Speaking before a group that included 13 former holders of the mile record in 1994, Dr. Roger Bannister, the first to break the 4-minute mile, summed it up:

". . . we forget the pain and the fatigue and lashing yourself to try harder next time and next, illness and injury, real and sometimes imagined, the castigation of the press and coaches—all these fade away, because memory is kind. We remember the good times, the sun on our backs, running through the beauty of the countryside, running thousands and thousands of miles . . . for us, no matter what life may bring, whatever subsequent shadows there may be, no one can strip us of these memories."

CHRONOLOGY

776 B.C.	First written record of an Olympic race.
1873	College track competition begins in U. S.
1888	Amateur Athletic Union is formed.
1896	First modern Olympics takes place in Athens.
1932	Babe Didrikson wins AAU national team championship as one-person team.
1936	Jesse Owens wins four gold medals at Olympics in Berlin.
1940	Cornelius Warmerdam is the first to clear 15 feet in the pole vault.
1954	Roger Bannister runs first mile in under 4 minutes.
1968	Bob Beamon is the first to clear 29 feet in the long jump.
1997	Daniel Komen of Kenya becomes the first man to run 2 miles in under 8 minutes with 1-mile laps of 3:59.2 and 3:59.4. He repeats the feat a year later.
2002	Tim Montgomery earns the title of "World's Fastest Man" by running the 100-meter in a world record time of 9.78 seconds.

OLYMPIC GLOSSARY

Meter A meter is 10 percent longer than a yard; thus, 100 meters would equal about 110 yards. Olympic races are 100, 200, 400, 800, 1,500, 5,000, and 10,000 meters.

Marathon The marathon distance is 26 miles, 385 yards, which, according to legend, is the distance run by Pheidippides, a professional Greek messenger 2,500 years ago, to carry the news of a Greek victory over the Persians from the battlefield at Marathon to Athens. The story, for which there is no evidence, has the runner shouting, "Be joyful! We win!" then dropping dead from exhaustion. The marathon may begin in or outside a stadium; it ends at a finish line in the stadium after traversing roads and countryside. There are water and refreshment stands along the way, and medical checkups are available.

Relays Relays are run by four-person teams. After the start, each runner may use a running start while taking the baton from the preceding runner.

High Jump Each jumper competes until three successive misses. They must take off from one foot. The crossbar may be touched as long as it does not fall.

Pole Vault Poles may be of any length and made of any material. Rules are basically the same as for the high jump.

Long Jump The jump must be launched from behind the far edge of the takeoff board. It is measured to the nearest contact of the body in the sand where the jumper lands.

Triple Jump Also known as the hop, skip, and jump. it is a long jump preceded by a hop and a step.

Shot Put A 16-pound ball of brass or iron must be put from shoulder height, not thrown, while staying within a circle.

Hammer Throw The hammer is a 16-pound metal sphere attached to a grip by a steel spring wire. It is thrown from a circle. Most throwers spin three or four times before releasing it.

Javelin Throw A javelin is a spear of wood or metal, weighing not quite two pounds, and a little more than $8 \frac{1}{2}$ feet long. The thrower gets a running start. The metal tip must stick in the ground when it lands.

Hurdles Various distances run with 10 hurdles each $3 \frac{1}{2}$ feet high to be cleared.

3,000-Meter Steeplechase Runners encounter 28 solid hurdles each 3 feet high, and 7 water jumps consisting of ponds on the far side of hedges 12 feet long and about 2 feet thick.

20,000-Meter Walk Walking races go back many centuries. One foot must be on the ground at all times. Most walking races occur on a track; Olympic events often go on main roads for the distance of almost 12 miles.

Discus A flat platter made of metal and wood, it weighs about 4 pounds for men, and a little over 2 pounds for women. The thrower holds it in one hand, spins once, and hurls it with a sidearm motion.

Decathlon Ten events done over two days: first day 100-meter run, long jump, shot put, high jump, and 400-meter run; second day 110-meter high hurdles, discus throw, pole vault, javelin throw, and 1,500-meter run.

FURTHER READING

Ashe, Arthur R. Jr. *A Hard Road to Glory: Track & Field.* New York: Amistad Press, 1993.

Durant, John. *Highlights of the Olympics.* New York: Hastings House, 1973.

Lewis, Carl. *Inside Track.* New York: Simon & Schuster, 1990.

Lynn, Elizabeth A. *Babe Didrikson Zaharias.* Philadelphia: Chelsea House, 1989.

Rennert, Rick. *Jesse Owens.* Philadelphia: Chelsea House, 1992.

Sullivan, George. *Great Lives: Sports.* New York: Macmillan, 1988.

Wallechinsky, David. *The Complete Book of the Summer Olympics.* Boston: Little, Brown and Company, 1996.

INDEX

PICTURE CREDITS Library of Congress: pp. 6, 9, 12, 25, 32, 37, 42; National Archives: pp. 2, 39, 40, 60; New York Public Library: pp. 15, 18, 20, 26, 27, 31; Boston Public Library: p. 28; AP/Wide World: pp. 34, 43, 44, 46, 49, 52, 54, 57.

NORMAN L. MACHT is the author of more than 25 books, 20 of them for Chelsea House Publishers. He is also the coauthor of biographies of former ballplayers Dick Bartell and Rex Barney, and is a member of the Society for American Baseball Research. He is the president of Choptank Syndicate, Inc. and lives in Baltimore, Maryland.